Presented to

_____

By

_____

On

_____

"The Holy Spirit will come upon you, and the
power of the Most High will overshadow you;
therefore, the child to be born will be holy; he
will be called Son of God."

Luke 1:35

God's Treasure
A Catholic Baby's Record Book

Illustrated by
Kathy Fincher

Regina
Press

THE REGINA PRESS
77 West End Road
Totowa, New Jersey 07512
www.reginapress.com

ISBN# 9780882711492

Printed in China.
CPSIA   December 2017   10 9 8 7 6 5 4 3 2 L/P

Table of Contents

My Birth Certificate

And Jesus called to them, saying "Let the
little children come to me, and do not hinder
them, for to such belongs the kingdom of God."
Luke 18:16

My Birth

My name is _____

I was born at _____ o'clock _____ M

on _____ Date

at _____ Place

in _____ City, State

Doctor _____

Pediatrician _____

Nurses _____

I weighed _____ lbs. _____ ozs.

and measured _____ inches _____

My hair was _____ and my eyes were _____

I was named _____

because _____

_____

I was the _____ child

of (Father) _____

and of (Mother) _____

My home was at _____

_____

_____

My First Photograph

"And a little child shall lead them."
Isaiah 11:16

Visitors and Gifts

Name	Gift

My Family

Great-Great Grandmother

_____

Great-Great Grandfather

_____

Great Grandmother

_____

Great Grandfather

_____

Grandmother

_____

Grandfather

_____

Mother

_____

Great-Great Grandmother

_____

Great-Great Grandfather

_____

Great Grandmother

_____

Great Grandfather

_____

Grandmother

_____

Grandfather

_____

Father

_____

Baby

_____

My Relatives

Name	Relationship

I have baptized you in water; He will baptize you in the Holy Spirit.

Mark 1:8

My Baptism

I received the Sacrament of Baptism on

_____ Date

at _____ church

in _____ ,

Parish _____

The Reverend _____

baptized me and my godfather,

_____

and my godmother,

_____

sponsored me.

These friends and relatives were present:

Grandpa & Grandma Blevins

GRANDPA Connor

Great Grandma Connor

17

"O sing to the Lord a new song, for he has done marvelous things."

Psalm 98:1

My Early Development

MEMORABLE FIRSTS   Date

Held my head up _____

Turned my head _____

Had a bath _____

Recognized my mother _____

Recognized my father _____

Rolled over _____

Ate solid food _____

Recognized objects _____

Sat up _____

Crawled on all fours _____

Pulled myself up _____

Steps taken _____

Sounds uttered _____

Words spoken _____

Haircut _____

Tooth _____

Drew a picture _____

Began to count _____

Playmates _____

_____

OTHER FIRSTS _____

_____

_____

"Make a joyful noise to the Lord, all the earth."
Psalm 100:1

My Favorite Things

Toys _____

_____

_____

Clothes _____

_____

Pets _____

_____

Games _____

_____

Stories _____

_____

Prayers _____

_____

Songs _____

_____

_____

T.V. Show _____

_____

_____

Playmates _____

_____

_____

Other Favorites _____

_____

"Rejoice always, praying without ceasing,
Give thanks in all circumstances."

Ephesians 5:16

Other Memorable Firsts

My Mother and Father taught me how to pray as a child.
This is the first prayer I ever learned.

_____

_____

In time, I learned these important prayers.

_____ Age_____

_____ Age_____

_____ Age_____

On _____ at the age of _____
my Mother and Father brought me to _____
_____ church

in _____

On _____ at the age of_____
I began my religious education at _____
_____ school

in _____

I was in _____ grade and my teacher was _____

I attended my first Mass on _____
at _____ church

in _____

The Reverend _____ was the celebrant.

I was _____ years old and these members of the family
were present: _____

Other Sacraments
I Have Received

Reconciliation

I received the Sacrament of Reconciliation at the age of
_____ on _____
at _____ church
in _____.
The Reverend _____ heard my confession.

Confirmation

I became a soldier of Christ on _____
at _____ church
in _____.
I was _____ years old.
Bishop_____ confirmed me
and _____ was my sponsor.
I took the name of _____
in Confirmation.
These members of my family were present: _____

_____

_____

_____

_____

First Holy Communion

I received Jesus in the Eucharist for the first time on

at _____ church

in _____ parish.

I was _____ years old.

The Reverend _____ celebrated the Mass,

and The Reverend _____

gave me communion.

These members of my family were present: _____

_____

_____

_____

_____

_____

_____

_____

_____

_____

This day in David's city a savior has been
born to you, the Messiah and Lord.

Luke 2:11

My First
Christmas

_____

_____

_____

_____

_____

_____

_____

_____

_____

_____

_____

_____

_____

_____

_____

_____

_____

_____

_____

_____

_____

"For the love of christ urges us on."
II Corinthians 5:14

My Travels and Vacations

"We are God's children now, what we will be
has not been revealed."

I John 3:2

My First Birthday

Second Birthday

_____

_____

_____

_____

_____

_____

Third Birthday

_____

_____

_____

_____

_____

Fourth Birthday

_____

_____

_____

_____

_____

_____

Fifth Birthday

_____
_____
_____
_____
_____
_____

Sixth Birthday

_____
_____
_____
_____
_____
_____
_____

Seventh Birthday

_____
_____
_____
_____
_____

_____

He grew in wisdom and age and
grace before God and men.

Luke 2:52

My Growth chart

Pounds and Ounces   Feet and Inches

Birth _____   _____

1 Month _____   _____

2 Months _____   _____

3 Months _____   _____

4 Months _____   _____

5 Months _____   _____

6 Months _____   _____

7 Months _____   _____

8 Months _____   _____

9 Months _____   _____

10 Months _____   _____

11 Months _____   _____

1 Year _____   _____

1½ Years _____   _____

2 Years _____   _____

2½ Years _____   _____

3 Years _____   _____

3½ Years _____   _____

4 Years _____   _____

5 Years _____   _____

6 Years _____   _____

7 Years _____   _____

"Bless the Lord, O my soul."
Psalm 103:22

My Dental Chart

Central Incisor, 7 ½ months

Lateral Incisor, 9 months

Cuspid, 18 months

First Molar, 14 months

Second Molar, 24 months

First Permanent Molar, 6 years

First Permanent Molar, 6 years

Second Molar, 20 months

First Molar, 12 months

Cuspid, 16 months

Lateral Incisor, 7 months

Central Incisor, 6 months

Visits to the Dentist

Date	Age	Doctor's Name

My Illnesses

Date	Age	Doctor's Name

My Medical Record

Immunizations	Date of Boosters	Series Completed	Doctor's Name
Diphtheria			
dpt { Tetanus			
Whooping Cough			
Measles			
mmr { Mumps			
Rubella			
Polio			
Other			

Tests		Date	Doctor's Name
Tuberculin			
Other			

Blood Type _____

Allergies	Doctor's Name	Remarks

"For I am the Lord who heals you."
Exodus 15:26

My Visits
to the Doctor

Date	Age	Remarks

"Happy are those who find wisdom, and those who get understanding... She is a tree of life to those."

Proverbs 3:13

My Schooling

Nursery School

_____
_____
_____
_____
_____
_____
_____

Kindergarten

_____
_____
_____
_____
_____
_____
_____
_____
_____

First Grade

_____
_____
_____
_____
_____
_____

Second Grade

_____
_____
_____
_____
_____
_____

Third Grade

_____
_____
_____
_____
_____
_____

Fourth Grade

_____
_____
_____
_____
_____
_____
_____

Fifth Grade

_____
_____
_____
_____
_____
_____

Sixth Grade

_____
_____
_____
_____
_____
_____
_____
_____